Nature's WORST Parents

BEASTLY Birds

Alix Wood

Gareth Stevens PUBLISHING

Please visit our website, www.garethstevens.com. For a free color catalog of all our high-quality books, call toll free 1-800-542-2595 or fax 1-877-542-2596.

Cataloging-in-Publication Data
Names: Wood, Alix.
Title: Beastly birds / Alix Wood.
Description: Buffalo, NY : Gareth Stevens Publishing, 2027. |
Series: Nature's worst parents | Includes glossary and index.
Identifiers: ISBN 9781482477627 (pbk.) | ISBN 9781482477634 (library bound) |
ISBN 9781482477641 (ebook)
Subjects: LCSH: Birds--Juvenile literature. |
Classification: LCC QL697.W65 2027 | DDC 598.03--dc23

Published in 2027 by
Gareth Stevens Publishing
2544 Clinton St.
Buffalo, NY 14224

Designed and written by Alix Wood

Picture Credits: all illustrations © Alix Wood;

Photo credits; Cover, 6, 7, 8 bottom, 9, 10, 11, 12, 16 bottom, 18, 20 right, 22, 23, 24, 25, 26, 27, 29, 30, 31 left © AdobeStock Images; 5 © Princepauljoy/Creative Commons; 8 top © Shuhari/Creative Commons; 14 © Juan Maria Raggioon/Creative Commons; 16 top © Awayk3n/Creative Commons; 20 left © Dion Art/Creative Commons; 23 © NRKNatur/Creative Commons; 28 © William Kreijkes/Creative Commons; 31 right © Soulwrite Empire/Creative Commons

Printed in China
CPSIA compliance information: Batch #QS27GS: For further information contact Gareth Stevens at 1-800-542-2595.

Find us on

Contents

ALL ABOUT BIRDS

Birds are found in every country of the world and are all different sizes and colors. There are over 10,000 different types of birds! Most birds are great parents.

IS IT A BIRD? Does it ...

... lay eggs?
... have a bill or beak?
... have two legs?
... have wings?
... have feathers?

If the answer to all these is "Yes," then it's a bird.

All birds have wings, but not all birds can fly.

Some seabirds, such as puffins, can swim AND fly.

Ostriches are too heavy to fly, but they can run fast.

Tiny hummingbirds can hover in midair by moving their wings very fast.

Penguins can't fly, but they are great swimmers.

Most birds make a nest for the mom to lay her eggs in. Both mom and dad may care for and feed the chicks.

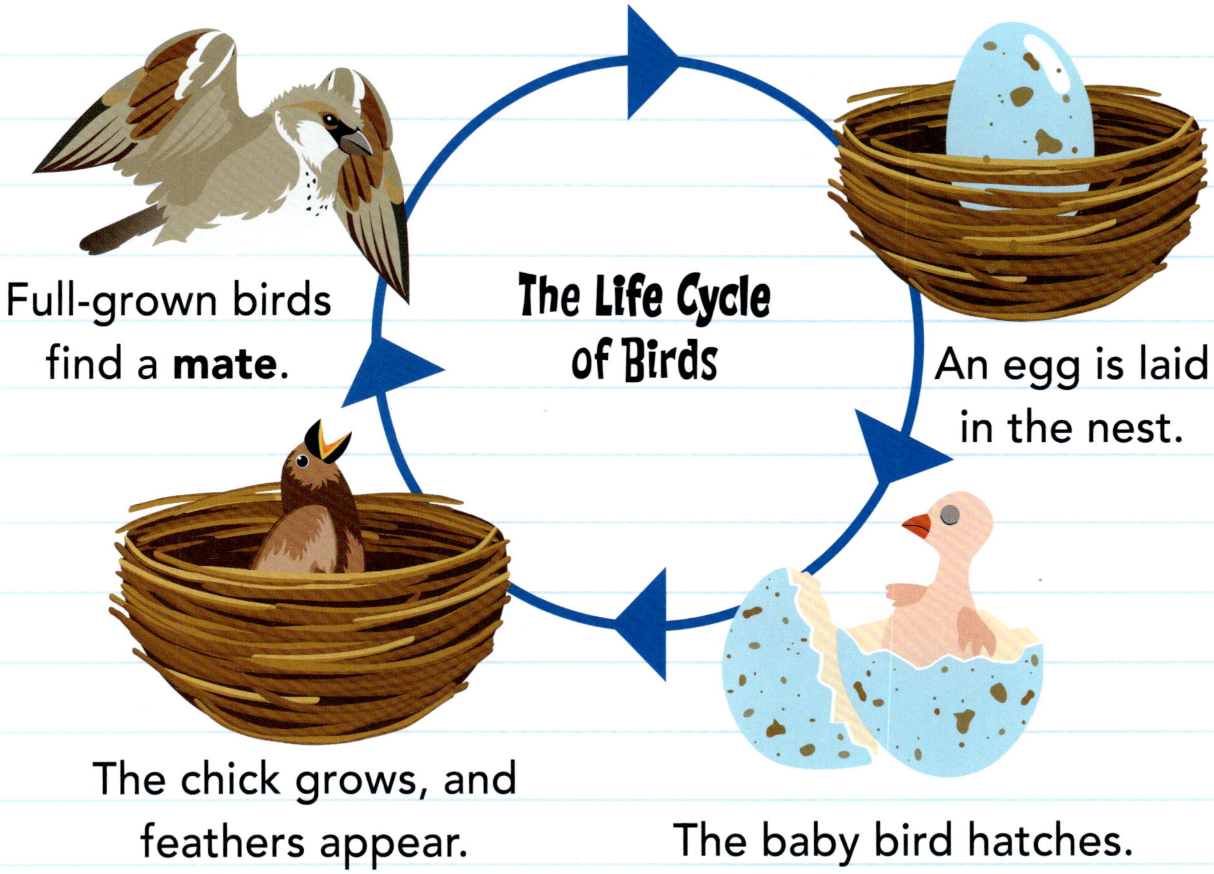

Paradise flycatchers are good parents. They make cute nests using twigs and spider webs.

Bird nests may be a simple hole in the sand, or an amazing woven basket. Birds sit on the eggs in their nest until the chicks hatch.

Birds CAN be great parents, but they also do some pretty mean things!

Cuckoos

Cuckoos have a strange style of parenting. The female cuckoo sneaks into another bird's nest to lay her eggs. They often lay eggs in reed warbler, dunnock, and crow nests.

The cuckoo may push one of the **host bird**'s eggs out of the nest, so the new egg looks less suspicious.

WHAT?

The cuckoo chick hatches first. Then it shoves all the other eggs out of the nest!

a cuckoo chick pushing a reed warbler egg out of the nest

Why Do They Do That?

Finding food and defending a nest takes a lot of energy. It can even get a parent injured or killed. Tricking someone else into doing the work makes life much easier.

Crow eggs and chicks are too large to push and bully, so some crow chicks survive a cuckoo invasion.

Cuckoos actually help the crows. Cuckoo chicks squirt a bad-tasting substance at predators, which drives them away!

Emus

An emu mom lays between five and fifteen very large, thick-shelled, green eggs. Laying that many big eggs does take some effort. So, she leaves the rest to dad!

Why Do They Do That?

Emu dads are just great dads! The dad builds a comfortable, flat nest of sticks on the ground. Then, he carefully lines it with grass and leaves.

The emu dad doesn't eat or drink for eight weeks while he sits on the eggs. He loses a third of his body weight. He survives by drinking any drops of dew he can reach from the nest!

Different emu moms may lay their eggs in a dad's nest. He can end up with as many as 25 chicks to care for!

The emu dad feeds and protects the chicks for over six months. He ruffles his feathers, kicks, and grunts at any emus who come close, including mom.

WHAT?

A charging emu mom can harm their own chicks with an accidental kick. They do not have the dad's protective instinct.

House Sparrows

Little house sparrow moms and dads both usually help raise their babies. The mom sits on the eggs, while the dad guards the nest and brings her food.

Mom will leave the nest for a drink and a bathroom break sometimes.

Mom and dad both feed the chicks once they hatch. Studies have shown that if mom was away too long during her nest breaks, the dad gets mad and won't help as much!

DAD MAY NOT FEED HIS CHICKS IF HE'S FIGHTING WITH MOM!

Why Do They Do That?

Both parents are kept busy finding food and guarding the nest from predators. The male sparrow does most of the work, so chicks only survive if he is a good dad. The female needs to rest and get herself strong enough to lay more eggs.

Like many birds, if house sparrows have too many beaks to feed, they may kill the weaker chicks. This gives their other chicks a better chance of survival.

WHAT?

A house sparrow mom may kill chicks in another sparrow mom's nest. Why? She kills other chicks that her mate may be the father of, so he only looks after her chicks!

Shoebills

These strange-looking birds stand around 5 feet (1.5 m) tall and have huge, heavy beaks. Shoebill moms usually lay two eggs. Mom and dad are really great parents, to ONE of their chicks!

Parents carry water and fish back to the nest in their large beaks.

Shoebills only feed their healthiest chick!

WHAT?

The two shoebill eggs are laid a few days apart. The chick that hatches from the first egg has a few days' growth before the chick from the second egg hatches. This larger chick attacks, and sometimes kills, its smaller **sibling**.

If the younger chick survives the attack, the shoebill parents guide the stronger chick away and **abandon** the youngest one!

Why Do They Do That?

Shoebill chicks need a lot of food to grow from a small chick into a large adult. They need a lot of care too. Their large beaks can cause them to topple over! Shoebill parents figure it is better to concentrate on raising just one needy chick.

Hooded Grebes

When a mom and dad hooded grebe first meet they do a **courtship** dance. They press their chests together and lift themselves up above the water. Then they shake their heads and swim in circles, moving their necks backward and forward.

The happy couple builds a floating nest from plants found in the water. Then, the female lays two eggs.

hooded grebe on her nest

Predators such as gulls, mink, and birds of prey may eat grebe eggs. The grebes guard them well. So far, hooded grebes are GREAT parents.

WHAT?

When the first egg hatches, the grebes abandon the second egg. If by a miracle both chicks hatch at exactly the same time, the parents will raise both chicks.

One parent carries the lucky first chick on its back. The other parent catches food for them.

FIRST TO HATCH WINS!

Why Do They Do That?

The second egg is just a spare, in case the first egg doesn't hatch. Laying two eggs makes it more likely that one of the eggs will produce a healthy chick.

Scientists protecting hooded grebes sometimes rescue abandoned eggs and raise the chicks themselves!

Black Eagles

Huge, soaring black eagles work hard building a nest high up in a tree or on a cliff. Then, mom lays two eggs in the nest.

The mom and dad both take turns sitting on the eggs. They keep the eggs warm until both chicks hatch.

The two eggs are laid a few days apart. The chick that hatches first will be bigger and stronger than the second one.

Dad eagle hunts for food. Mom guards the nest and feeds the chicks the food that he brings.

The stronger chick will steal any food mom tries to give to the smaller chick. It bullies its sibling too. Eventually, the weaker chick will usually die.

WHAT?

When the parents return to find one dead chick, they don't seem to mind. It means there is one less beak to feed. In fact, they feed the dead chick to the remaining chick! Black eagles don't waste good food!

Why Do They Do That?

The dead chick makes a good snack, and eating it helps clean up the nest too.

Barn Owls

Barn owls usually lay two eggs, one a few days after the first. The larger chick is always fed first. If there is plenty of prey, both owlets will survive.

If food is hard to find, the younger one will starve. Then, it becomes food for the older owlet.

THE KIDS MAKE A GREAT SNACK!

Why Do They Do That?

The barn owls' second egg is laid just in case the first chick dies. If food is scarce, the second chick makes a nice snack for the first.

WHAT?

Barn owl chicks may kill and eat each other if food is scarce. Last year's chick may even come back to their old nest to snack on this year's chicks!

Mom and dad barn owl can accidentally kill a chick as they fly in and out of their nest too.

Coots

Most birds' chicks have feathers that blend in with their surroundings. This helps them hide from predators. Coot chicks have crazy orange feathers. Why? Mom and dad tend to feed the most colorful chick!

Why Do They Do That?

The youngest chicks have the most colorful feathers. Their feathers fade after around six days. Feeding the most colorful chicks means the younger chicks are fed the most. The faded chicks are older, so they already have a good chance of survival.

Coots sneakily lay eggs in other coots' nests if those nests have fewer eggs than their own nest. Why?

Chicks in an emptier nest have less competition for food. Sneaky egg laying gives those chicks a better chance of survival.

While one coot is laying eggs in another coot's nest, other coots may sneak over and lay their eggs in her nest!

WHAT?

If coots have too many chicks to care for, they drown, peck, or starve the weakest of their chicks to death.

Common Murre

These birds live life on the edge. They nest, tightly packed, on steep coastal ledges and cliffs. This is a very difficult place to keep an egg, or a tiny chick, safe.

WE LAY OUR EGGS ON A CLIFF FACE!

Why Do They Do That?

The crowded, dangerous cliffs can lead to breakages, but the eggs are safer from predators.

The murre's pointy eggs are more stable on sloping cliffs. More of the egg touches the ground than with a normal egg.

At just three weeks old, murre chicks must leave the cliffs and join dad in the water below. However, their feathers are not developed enough to allow them to fly!

Luckily, murre chicks aren't afraid of a little cliff diving. They simply hurl themselves off the cliffs and plummet toward the water.

WHAT?

Luckily, the chicks are so light and fluffy that they usually bounce if they hit the rocks on the way down.

a murre chick throwing itself off a cliff

Australian Brush Turkeys

Male brush turkeys build huge nest mounds that are the size of a small car! This attracts female brush turkeys, who lay eggs in his nest.

a male brush turkey busy building his nest

The nest may hold up to 150 eggs! The eggs are buried around 2 to 2.5 feet (60 to 80 cm) deep inside the mound.

Why Do They Do That?

The plant matter in the giant nest starts to rot, which creates heat. The heat keeps the eggs warm, so the turkeys don't need to sit on them. Dad sticks his beak in the mound to check the temperature. He adds material if the nest is too cool, or takes material away if it gets too hot.

WHAT?

Mom and dad don't look after the chicks AT ALL. The tiny chicks must find their own food and keep out of danger. Luckily, the chicks are born fully-feathered and can fly after just a few hours.

The chicks have strong legs. They need them to dig their way out of their nest!

Nazca Boobies

"Booby" comes from the Spanish word "bobo," meaning clown. Boobies got their name because the birds are clumsy. It's not a great idea to lay your eggs on a cliff face if you're clumsy.

WE LAY OUR EGGS ON CLIFFS AND LET THE KIDS FIGHT TO THE DEATH!

Booby moms usually lay two eggs. The mom and dad take turns keeping them warm. They use their big, webbed feet to hold the eggs close to their body.

Once hatched, the older chick pushes the younger one out of the nest. Mom and dad may even peck and stamp on the chick too!

Why Do They Do That?

Laying two eggs gives the parents a better chance of having one heathy chick. That is because 25 to 50 percent of booby eggs fail to hatch. Once one healthy chick arrives, boobies don't want to look after any more.

WHAT?

Boobies swallow, and then throw up, their kid's food! This may seem gross, but it keeps their food from being stolen by other birds as they fly back to the nest.

A booby parent **regurgitates** fish into their chick's mouth.

Hoopoes

Hoopoes eat large insects. During some times of year, there are too many to eat all at once. If only they could store food for when it runs low! Hoopoes have come up with a gruesome solution! They raise some chicks as food for the others.

I CREATE A STORE CUPBOARD—OF CHICKS!

Why Do They Do That?

The "chick larder" does solve a problem. Hoopoes use the extra energy they get from eating so much food to produce more eggs. It's a clever way of storing the food! Chicks with a chick food store have a better chance of survival.

Hoopoes' long, curved beaks are perfect for eating insects. They aren't as ideal for killing chicks. So, hoopoes don't bother. They just push whole, live "larder" chicks into their favored chicks' mouths!

These eggs may become a chick larder.

Male hoopoes use their long beaks to stab each other when they fight.

WHAT?

Hoopoe moms produce a nasty-smelling liquid that smells like rotten meat. They rub the liquid into their chicks' feathers. The smell helps keep predators and parasites away. It may also protect the chicks from germs.

Hoopoe chicks can look after themselves. They hiss and strike predators with a wing or beak. If that doesn't work, they fire poop at them!

Glossary

abandon To leave a place, thing, or person.

courtship Behavior that has the aim of attracting a mate.

host bird The bird that a parasite bird lives with, and from which it gets its food.

life cycle A series of changes that an organism will go through throughout its life.

mate An animal's breeding partner.

regurgitates Brings swallowed food up again to the mouth.

predators Animals that hunt, kill, and eat other animals

sibling A brother or sister.

Index